D0340691

KABBALAH ON green

© 2008 Kabbalah Centre International, Inc.

All rights reserved. No part of this publication may be reproduced or transmitted in any form or by any means, electronic or mechanical, including photocopying, recording, or by any information storage and retrieval system, without permission in writing from the publisher, except by a reviewer who wishes to quote brief passages in connection with a review written for inclusion in a magazine, newspaper, or broadcast.

Kabbalah Publishing is a registered DBA of
Kabbalah Centre International, Inc.

For further information:

The Kabbalah Centre
155 E. 48th St., New York, NY 10017
1062 S. Robertson Blvd., Los Angeles, CA 90035

1.800.Kabbalah www.kabbalah.com

First Edition
February 2008
Printed in Canada
ISBN10: 1-57189-595-7
ISBN13: 978-1-57189-595-0

Design: HL Design (Hyun Min Lee) www.hldesignco.com

100%

KABBALAH ON
green

CONSCIOUSNESS AND
THE ENVIRONMENT

YEHUDA BERG

DEDICATION

This book and all the Light that it reveals is dedicated to our magnificent planet in all its glory. May it reach its purpose and perfection with our joined souls of humanity.

With Love and Awe,

Yehuda

TABLE OF CONTENTS

ACKNOWLEDGMENTS

To the people who make my life better each and every day: my parents, the Rav and Karen; my brother Michael; my wife Michal and our children.

Chapter One

Al Gore and clean versus green

HEARTBREAK

Gore got it. Gore got it real good. No, I am not referring to the election that Al Gore lost. Then again, I am. Nor am I referring to a Presidency that some say was stolen out from under Gore's feet. Then again, I am.

When I say Gore got it, I mean Gore understood what life is all about. I'm not going to say if it was conscious or subconscious on Gore's part; but Gore got what life is all about because, for whatever reason, destiny put him in a unique place on election night. And fate put him there again the night when he conceded the election. That was the night Gore got green—though why this is so will probably shock you. I'll explain shortly.

It was, without question, the greatest night in Al Gore's life—though he probably did not know it. I pray he knows it now. And I pray that we know it by the end of this book. Not for Al's sake. For *our* sake. For *your* sake. The fact is, this has nothing at all to do with Al Gore. But it has everything to do with Al Gore's *actions*.

Once we understand what really happened to Al Gore, once we understand what it really means to either *clean up* or *green up* our world, we will complete the transformation of our Earth in a manner that is miraculously simple—an ultra-smooth transition.

That is what this book is all about. It's about how to change the world, how to *green up* and *not clean up* our planet. This book is about creating Eden. Real world, real life, authentic. Forever.

But the manner in which we can accomplish this will turn your view of the world upside down. 360 degrees. And not one degree less. Once you do—once others do—green will be the new clean.

The Difference Between Clean and Green

The fact is, we are *not* here to *clean* up our world. We are here to green it up. Kabbalah is all about achieving green. In our hearts. In our souls. On our planet.

What's the difference between clean and green? Everything. Beyond what you might dare to imagine.

Make no mistake, if we don't wake up and discover the difference between clean versus green, we will continue cleaning up our messes until we reach the point where our mess finally cleans us up. And that will hurt. And that will be tragic. It'll be tragic because it didn't have to hurt. It didn't have to be that way. Not any more. Not now.

Allow me to explain. And please pay close attention and open up your heart. You will have to first *clean* away some of that misguided knowledge and social conditioning that you've acquired in order to get what I am about to tell you.

Here we go:

To *clean* is to deal with a dirty mess *after* it has already been made. You know the age-old advice—*Remember to clean up after yourself.*

The problem with cleaning is that it means the mess is already there, right in front of us. The mess is already an interruption in our life. Thus, we are dealing with symptoms and not the cause. Furthermore, the same issue that caused the mess to appear in the first place is going to repeat itself and lead us into another mess—sooner rather than later. The result? We wind up running around in circles, making a mess, then cleaning it up, making a new mess, then cleaning that one up as well.

Soon we start getting tired of all the cleaning. We're not giving 100% any more. And we're just not happy because we're spending more and more of our time cleaning instead of living. What do we do? We don't clean up as much as we did before. We just tidy things up. Now the mess starts to grow. And grow. Pretty soon the clutter overtakes us so we hire someone else to clean up for us. We pass our garbage onto others, hoping they'll clean up after us.

This pattern continues in every area of our life. We start handing over all of our personal garbage, and our physical garbage, and our emotional garbage. Before you know it life, all around us, becomes one giant trash can.

Guess what? Everyone else inevitably follows suit. Soon the city becomes a trash can. Then the nation becomes a trash can. Then the world becomes a trash can.

Now we're left with one single option because we've remained stuck in our *clean-it-up consciousness*. We bury the physical trash under the ground. We dump it into the ocean in order to clean up the neighborhoods. If we don't see it, it must not be there. We do the same internally. We dump our personal, emotional, and spiritual trash on the people we love—and also on the people we don't love—in order to clean ourselves up to improve our self-esteem.

Now everyone in our lives, and in this world, is walking around with all kinds of garbage deep inside of them. So everyone starts dumping on everyone.

We delude ourselves into thinking that we're cleaning ourselves up when, in fact, all of us are just exchanging our own garbage for someone else's. It feels good for a moment but soon we smell the stench of the other person's garbage and we realize we achieved nothing. So we look for someone else to exchange garbage with, still believing we are cleaning up.

The garbage continues to grow and it starts permeating our businesses and industries. The excess sewage and muck oozes and seeps into the media, the entertainment industry, the political arena, and organized religion. Finally, the garbage becomes so humongous that it spills out into the environment because there are no more places on Earth to hide it. Everyone is filled to the brim with garbage internally and all the external dumping grounds on Earth are filled to capacity.

Meanwhile, everyone and every industry continues exchanging their garbage, or relocating it because there is no place left to dump it, and the filth and stench magnify exponentially.

Now the water, the air, the trees, and the food supply become tainted and defiled, and they're now ready for the bin. Except there are no more bins, no more make-shift dumpsters to dump all this new waste. So there is but one option—it all explodes and implodes, self-destructing so that all the toxic wastes, noxious poisons, and radioactive refuse come apart. Their molecules and atoms are torn asunder so that they no longer exist in the form of garbage—like a Lego monster taken apart, piece by piece, so that the monster exists no more. The atoms, like the Lego pieces, are still present because atoms are immortal! But these atoms are no longer assembled into the putrid, foul, stinking chunks of matter that we call waste. All life on Earth vanishes as the molecules break apart. The Earth becomes a sea of atoms which are now free to establish brand new bonds with other atoms, thereby forming new molecules, new kinds of matter, and new kinds of life forms. Only if we are very lucky will those life forms be kind, thoughtful beings who never again make the fatal mistake of **trying to <u>clean</u> up this planet!**

THE ALTERNATIVE UNIVERSE

Perhaps you want to avoid this kind of gloomy ending to the story of humankind. We can. We will. Thus, I invite you to keep reading in order to see what Gore got. Once we grasp, we'll immediately get green. Intellectually, physically, *and—most important*—spiritually.

And Al, if you happen to be reading this, it is my sincere hope that you discover the true power of what you did so that you may continue to do so and win your own personal fight against Global Warming. That will help everyone. Beyond what anyone can imagine.

Before we discover what Gore got, let's examine our world and the nature of reality according to the oldest *green* environmentalists on the planet—the ancient kabbalists.

The kabbalists wrote many books on Kabbalah which serve to decipher the Bible and reveal wonderful secrets and mysteries embedded into its literal texts.

The most important work of Kabbalah is, without question, the *Zohar*, the book of Splendor. Composed some 2000 years ago, the *Zohar* says whoever reads the Bible literally is a fool. Thus, the *Zohar* unravels the Bible layer by layer to reveal stunning truths about the nature of reality, the meaning of life, and the value of the world and the environment in which we live. It's a lifetime study, so I will share the simplest insights of the *Zohar* that relate directly to the topic at hand. If you read with an open heart, you will detect the depth of wisdom concealed in even the simplest of ideas.

Chapter Two

interconnected

INTERCONNECTED

We are all interconnected. People—*and the planet*. This connection achieves its highest state through human consciousness. The biblical story of Genesis and the kabbalists of history tell us that the entire vegetable kingdom—including trees, bushes, flowers, plants—were literally in a state of potential, a state of suspended animation when they were originally created by the force we humans call God. However, only after the birth of man—*human consciousness*—did these other kingdoms become animate and alive.

The underlying lesson behind this ancient kabbalistic insight concerns humankind's profound impact and influence on the entire planet. It is our actions and consciousness that either maintain or disturb that natural balance of the Earth, environmentally and socially. It is human hatred, intolerance, negative speech, slander, lying, and arguing between neighbors, families, nations, and religions that inevitably blanket the environment with negative energy. This is the ultimate cause that leads to the degradation of the environment. Pollution, carbon emissions, toxic waste are merely the effects born out of our negative consciousness and intolerant behavior toward one another.

It is the constant hatred, killing, murder, injustice, the consciousness of despair and anguish in human society which creates a dark and disturbing energy field around the globe. This negatively-charged field is why the whole planet begins to fall apart, little by little, step by step in a domino chain reaction.

The Domino Effect
Science discovers a hole in the ozone layer that inevitably allows too much ultraviolet radiation to seep into the atmosphere. This leads to an increase in skin cancer and, thus, more emotional pain and distress amongst the families that are afflicted. The increased radiation, in turn, engenders global warming, which causes the climate to become less stable, resulting in too much rain in one area of the planet and too little rain in another. This leads to more deserts from the

lack of rain, more swamps and floods where the rains run rampant.

As icebergs melt and torrential rains increase, cities are suddenly facing the threat of sinking under the sea. Large areas of fertile land that could once grow an abundance of food for millions of people no longer can as they are turning to sand and dust.

According to the *Zohar*, all this degradation and chain reaction of destruction is a result of the pain that humankind injects into the world. The pain we inflict upon one another is the first domino.

The Oneness of it All

Humankind, mountains, lakes, rivers, wildlife, and even the clouds and ozone layer, are all made up of one common substance—*atoms*. The only reason water looks different from a long-necked giraffe is because of the particular arrangement of its atoms. But at the most fundamental level of reality, there is zero difference between a bird in the sky and a child playing in the park. Toxic waste is made up of atoms and so are scented roses. What determines whether atoms form toxic waste or natural resources? Only human consciousness. The same way we have the power to take the letters L. E. V. I. and arrange them to either spell LIVE or EVIL, we possess the power to manipulate and sequence the atoms in our world to create either positive energy or negative. When our consciousness is negative, when we are mistreating others, the atoms in the mountains, rivers, and ozone layer are shifted out of sequence. Some of the atoms that "spell" ozone are rearranged into a different sequence. This is why the holes start appearing in the ozone layer. It first begins in the realm of human consciousness and then it appears as a physical effect. According to Kabbalah, it is consciousness that leads to drought. Famine. Tornadoes. Tsunamis. Exotic new viruses and bacteria.

Our consciousness interacts with the entire planet every moment of the day.

Lost Civilization

The *Zohar* tells us that this is not the first time in history that human behavior and negative consciousness destroyed the world. The famous story of the super-advanced civilization known as Atlantis is none other than a generation of the consciousness of Noah during the time of the Flood. The story of Atlantis first appeared in the writings of Plato. However, Plato was, without question, a student of Kabbalah. Sir Isaac Newton, the greatest of all scientists, himself wrote that Plato derived all of his ideas from the ancient kabbalists of his time. Furthermore, the great scientists and philosophers of the scientific revolution and the Renaissance agreed wholeheartedly with Newton.

According to Kabbalah, Atlantis is a fictional account of an actual event that took place in human history. The Flood. It was the collective self-centered fragmented consciousness of humankind that caused the waters of the Earth to fall out of balance and thus flood the planet. God did not inflict judgment upon the world.

Humankind inflicted the judgment by virtue of our collective negative behavior.

The *Zohar* describes a world very much like ours is today. The *Zohar* says the people of that time were mixing and cross-breeding the various animal species, trying to create new life forms. The sanctity and Divinity of sexual relationships was degraded into wanton selfish acts of abuse and decadence. And there was zero concern for the welfare of those who were impoverished. People were using advanced spiritual technologies, like Kabbalah, for selfish, self-centered purposes and this is why nature eventually rose up against them.

The story of Noah and Atlantis has returned. Our civilization is super-advanced, technologically speaking. It is these very advances that now threaten us in the form of nuclear war, bio-terrorism, new diseases and viruses, and of course global warming.

Ancient Ozone Layer

Two-thousand years ago the *Zohar* spoke of the ozone layer, describing it as the sheath that protects us from the sword. The *Zohar* described the sword as the sun, whose rays, if unsheathed (unfiltered) would destroy instead of protect and nurture. The *Zohar* warned us about drawing the sword from out of its sheath, in other words, allowing the sun's rays to enter our world directly without being filtered through the ozone.

It is our actions that determine if the sword is sheathed or not. And our actions are determined solely by our states of consciousness.

Atomic Origin

Kabbalah reveals that all of the atoms that embody our existence were originally bound up as one unified whole prior to the physical creation of the Universe. There was one single conscious entity. It was not atom but rather Adam. And Adam was actually a force of pure consciousness containing both male (+) and female (–) aspects of energy. This is the mystery underlying the phrase *Adam and Eve*.

It was God who created this singular force of consciousness. At the moment of the Big Bang—which kabbalists described 2000 years before modern physics—this one force of consciousness shattered into countless miniaturized particles of consciousness. These are the atoms that comprise our world. The electron pertains to Eve, whereas the proton corresponds to Adam. The neutron is the free will that we possess to either share or receive, to be selfless or selfish. The world and our environment merely respond to the choices we make.

Kabbalists explain that a tree, a river, the sky, and the grocery clerk who checks you out at the supermarket are really made up of the same stuff—atoms—and thus are absolutely one on a deeper level of reality. The grocery clerk and the grass on your front lawn were all part of the original single force of consciousness called Adam. Hence, we are not just a brother or a sister to other people or to the rainforests and lakes that are part of this planet. We are, unquestionably, one being. One entity. One single consciousness. We are limbs of one another. Born at the same time. Conceived at the same time. We merely shattered into individual particles of consciousness, creating the illusion of many. In the physical reality there is space between the shattered pieces of consciousness and this is why we do not recognize the underlying unity. Each of us wears a masquerade that creates the illusion that we are separate and distinct from one another. That masquerade is the body and it projects the illusion that I am different and disconnected from my neighbor, different and disconnected from the trees and mountains.

Happiness is Wholeness (*Holiness*)

Simple unity is our origin. Unity is our truth. Therefore, a human being cannot achieve total happiness and fulfillment without first being an integral part of the world in heart, mind, and soul. When we recognize the profound unity, we automatically refrain from intolerance toward our neighbor and from carelessness toward our environment. Incredibly, this is done out of self-interest. Namely, one realizes that one cannot attain happiness without first caring for one's friends and environment. Why? We recognize them as extensions of our own self. Morals, ethics, and the so-called *greater* good are not the motivation behind our new level of consciousness and behavior. On the contrary, it is pure self-interest that inspires loving behavior toward other people and the planet.

Human beings cannot feel contented if they do not feel whole. Our emptiness inside is due to our lack of connection to the whole world around us—not because we are lacking in material items or emotional possessions. We can never *receive* anything physical or non-physical that will remove our lack and emptiness. That is a backwards approach. The way to remove our emptiness is to extend ourselves *outward* and connect to the whole. When we connect and embrace the whole around us, we feel whole and contented within.

For this reason, the kabbalists teach us that it is imperative for every individual to live life as though the entire world were created just for him or her. Likewise, individuals must also, at the same time, live their lives as though they were created for one singular purpose—to serve the whole world. Possessing both forms of consciousness at the same time is the key to feeling whole, being whole, and being truly happy. This ancient kabbalistic truth is found in two contemporary schools of thought known as anthropocentricism and biocentrism. According to anthropocentricism, humankind is central and we are stewards of the planet. Accordingly, we should serve the planet, protect and nurture the environment, for this is what sustains us. The opposite school of thought is biocentrism, which states that every part of nature has a right to exist without any connection to humans whatsoever. The world exists and humans should not disturb it.

Kabbalistically, truth emerges when two opposites are fused together. In other words, truth is attained by synthesizing both schools.

The Illusion of Disconnection

Kabbalah explains that the only thing that separates a human from a mountain is the intensity and degree of consciousness. This can be compared to the shattering of a plate. There is only one plate. When it shatters, it separates into individual pieces, some large, some small. But there is still just one plate. All the pieces originate from the same source and are of the same substance. This entire Earth, the inanimate, vegetable, animal, and human kingdoms, are shattered pieces of the one plate—the one conscious force called Adam.

Humankind is simply the biggest piece of the one shattered force of consciousness. But humankind is made up of the exact same particles of consciousness as the trees, birds, and waterfalls that populate the planet. To cut down a tree is to cut off your own limb. This is not a metaphor. This is an absolute truth. And because humankind represents the largest piece of the shattered consciousness, it is humans' behavior toward their fellow humans that has the greatest influence on the planet.

Controlling the Rights to Reality

In Genesis, God blesses Adam and Eve and tells them to be fruitful and multiply, to fill the Earth and conquer it. He gives them the responsibility to rule over the fish of the sea, the birds of the sky, and every living thing that moves on the Earth. God tells Adam and Eve that He has given them every plant bearing seed that is upon the face of the Earth, including every tree whose fruit yields a seed. And this, God says, will be used for food, to sustain life on the planet.

God tells us that human beings have the power to have dominion over all these species. But at the same time, all species have the right to use all of these resources for their own use. Humankind has no permission from God to stop any other species from earning its own livelihood and attaining its own sustenance.

God then takes Adam and places him in the infamous Garden of Eden to till it and to guard it. However, Kabbalah explains that we are not talking about a physical garden. The only objects spoken of in the

Garden of Eden are *The Tree of Life* and *the Tree of Knowledge*.

The last time I checked Yellowstone Park or any other major forest area, I never found such trees. I heard of sequoias, redwoods, and maple trees, but never a *Tree of Life*.

The kabbalists explain that the Garden of Eden, Adam, and the two Trees were not physical entities that we perceive with our five senses. This was a realm of pure consciousness. Yet, God still tells Adam to till the ground. If the Garden of Eden is a non-physical realm of consciousness, why does the Bible still mention the idea of *tilling the ground*, which is obviously physical?

The secret being conveyed is the power of human consciousness to influence and nurture the physical landscape of Earth. It is consciousness first, and physical actions second, that impact and influence our environment.

The Tree of Life refers to a state of consciousness where one recognizes and perceives the absolute oneness of reality. This is positive, sharing *Light* consciousness that nurtures and elevates everything it perceives.

The *Tree of Knowledge* consciousness refers to the limitations of the five senses and self-centered desires. This kind of consciousness only takes and never shares. It sees fragmentation and is blind to the elegant unity that binds all reality.

We are all born into this world with a consciousness rooted in the *Tree of Knowledge* reality. Our purpose in life is to elevate against gravity, as trees do, rising out of selfishness and self-centeredness to embrace the *Tree of Life* consciousness. As we elevate, so too does our environment. Likewise, as we descend into a lower state of consciousness, so too does our world.

The Sons of God

The *Zohar* explained some 2000 years ago that a person can be either a slave or a Son of God. Slaves are those who labor and carry a great burden. They will do the minimum amount of work, for they despise the very work that they do. People with slave consciousness will never achieve true happiness and fulfillment. They live in misery. They die in misery. They never claim their birthright, which is a complete connection to the whole, the Light of the Creator, and a life of deep fulfillment.

A higher level of existence is exemplified by individuals who work for a salary. They exert greater effort, for they know they can achieve a promotion and thus a higher salary. These kinds of individuals, however, will constantly display ego to counter the fact that they still serve and work under someone else. They have the ability to see a bit further than the slave and thus will work even harder to attain nicer things, more material wealth, a bigger home, and a more expensive car. They work harder because they see more personal rewards.

The highest level that one can achieve, according to the *Zohar*, is the grade known as the Son. These individuals know that they are an extension of the Creator and that the entire world belongs to God. Thus, they take responsibility for the entire planet and the entire Universe. They know everything belongs to the Father and thus everything also belongs to them, for they are the Son of the Father and therefore they belong to everything else. Even if there is no physical gain to be had, the Son still exerts great effort to care for the world. If something is amiss anywhere on the planet these kinds of individuals feel the pain, for it is a part of them, no different than a child feeling the pain of its parents or parents feeling the pain of their children.

If a tree in the rainforest is cut down, the Son feels the pain and attempts to heal it—not for personal gain, but to ease the pain within himself and within the tree, for both are limbs of one body. The tree is a child of God and so too is the Son. Thus, a tree in Brazil is as much a sibling to the Son as his own blood brother.

Kabbalistically, each of us has the potential to become a Son of God. We are all children of the Light, and achieving this state of consciousness is our ultimate objective and destiny.

We are born as slaves into this world, enslaved to our egos and selfish consciousness, otherwise known as the *Tree of Knowledge*. We are enslaved to other people's perception of us.

When we climb out of this state of existence, we attain the level known as the *Tree of Life* or, as it is referred to in the *Zohar*, "The Son of the Holy One, Blessed Be He."

To care and feel for every speck of matter on Earth is to be free from slavery and to find true fulfillment. To care for the whole is to become whole inside. A child starving in the world becomes my child. Not metaphorically, but literally. A child crying tears is the shedding of my own tears. A child suffering on the other side of the globe becomes my suffering. To feel the pain of the world is the ability to heal the pain of the world.

Thus, the maximum impact we can have on healing the rest of the environment is through the interactions and behavior between one human and another. In other words, since human consciousness is the strongest, most influential force on Earth, repairing and healing our interrelationships will yield the most dramatic results in the world around us. Feeling and healing the pain of others must become our primary focus. Healing others is what heals the planet. Feeling the pain of those who suffer is to heal the pain and devastation of the trees, the oceans, and the sky at the same time.

The Bible is clear on this matter. The section of the Bible known as Deuteronomy, chapter 11, says that humans' collective state of mind can either create drought or produce a year filled with the precise amount of rainwater necessary to enrich the Earth and feed the world. The Bible and Kabbalah also confirm that it is human consciousness that brings about earth-quakes and all other natural disasters.

Make no mistake—our inability to perceive the connection and our skepticism do not negate this ancient spiritual truth. One can disbelieve in gravity but remains under its influence nonetheless.

We must rise above these limitations and discover these higher truths so that we can heal the planet by healing one another.

TOO SIMPLE

Perhaps nowadays it is just too easy to say that a tree and a human are made up of the same atoms. This notion has become so readily accepted, an idea now learned in grade school, that the profundity of it goes right over our heads. We still treat the planet and people as if they were separate from us. The unity of our being—atoms—is an intellectual insight, but not one that we feel in our hearts and souls.

There is not one reader who would willfully flush toxic waste down his or her own throat in an effort to rid the world of such poisons. Yet we flush it into our lakes, we dump it into our rivers, never realizing that the lakes and rivers are made up of the exact same atoms as ourselves. We are all part of the one force of consciousness. Therefore, to dump toxic waste into a river is no different than dumping it down one's own throat. It is only the illusion of space and time that deceives us into believing that we are separate and distinct from our environment. Sooner or later, the poisons in our water will reach our very bodies. Time merely delays the inevitable. Space merely creates the illusion that a flowing river is separate from the blood that flows through my veins.

Let's examine this unity further so that it begins to sink in.

Chapter Three

the puzzle of creation

A WORK OF ART

Suppose we have a priceless work of art created by a renowned artist. The work of art is actually a magnificent painting, cut into a picture puzzle, and then fully assembled. This prized piece of art is framed and hung in a museum. When the puzzle is assembled and framed, it achieves its incalculable value. But suppose the puzzle is temporarily taken apart, separated into individual pieces. What happens if even a single piece of the puzzle is damaged? Even if the puzzle consists of 2000 puzzle pieces, if just one corner of one tiny piece is damaged or broken, the complete puzzle cannot be assembled. Consequently, its entire value is lost. Just like that. Is there any one piece, large or small, that is more important than another? No. If we damage 10 pieces, 1000 pieces or just one corner of one piece, does it matter? No. The entire work of art loses its value regardless.

Kabbalists tell us that Creation is a priceless puzzle. God created one entity. Only one. It is called Adam, a single force of consciousness that might also be called Atom. Adam (atom) was taken apart, like a picture puzzle, separated by space (our Universe), creating countless miniature Adams (atoms). These atoms reconfigured in different forms, creating the diversity that is our world. This took place so that we would not immediately recognize the priceless work of art that God created. It was left up to us to put the puzzle back together again. When we destroy a tree, kill an animal for sport, or dump poison into our lakes and rivers, it is akin to breaking another piece of the puzzle. One tiny broken puzzle piece prevents the perfection of all reality. So whether the damage we cause is massive or tiny, the result is the same. Perfection cannot be achieved. Thus, in terms of importance, even the tiniest of infractions against the environment, or against a single person, prevents the wholeness of perfection from being achieved. Thus, we should realize that even breaking a twig off a tree prevents perfection as much as a dumping toxic waste. Perfection means all the pieces must be whole.

One unkind, hurtful word to our spouse, friends or colleagues prevents the perfection of our world.

This is not to say that tons of toxic waste does not contribute *more* darkness than the purposely broken twig. It does. Kabbalah is also not saying that cheating, lying, robbing, and raping does not cause more damage than cursing at a friend. It does. But *both* are equally important in terms of *preventing* the final perfection and wholeness of our environment and world. Thus, we need to be mindful of all our actions, small and large. We need to strive for tolerance at every level of existence, for every conscious thought and act affects the whole around us and the whole within us.

For this reason, the Bible tells us that it is considered a felony to cut down a tree for sport or aesthetic purposes. Even when waging war against an enemy, the Bible says one must not fell a tree by ax. If a city is being captured during wartime, the trees must not be touched. Why? You are damaging the whole. One tree is an integral part of the puzzle of Creation.

Furthermore, you are negating the purpose of the other *puzzle* pieces that connect to this lone tree, like the birds who nest in it, the creatures who feed off it, the flora and fauna living in the tree.

A tree, according to the Bible, may be cut to build a home for one person. And we may eat of its fruits. But to ax a tree for sport or aesthetics is a crime and it corrupts the balance of nature.

By the way, the Bible is not condoning war. According to Kabbalah, war is being used as a metaphor to dramatically convey the importance of a single tree to all of Creation. In truth, there is only one war spoken of in the Bible, though it is purposely difficult to detect this when reading the Bible literally. The only war being fought in the Bible is the war within. The war against our own *Tree of Knowledge* consciousness which separates the rest of the world from our own being. That is the only enemy we came to defeat.

Screaming of the Trees

The Bible also tells us that when a single tree is being cut, it lets out a piercing scream that literally pulsates throughout the world, though it cannot be physically heard by human ears. If the cries of a lone tree tremble across the globe, just imagine the screams and anguished noise created by the daily devastation of the rainforests and the acres of trees that are being cut down every hour.

This biblical insight illustrates the sanctity and importance of every single piece of Creation and the dangers associated with wasting any part of it, large or small.

God's Nature

The kabbalists have pointed out that the numerical value of the Hebrew word for *nature* is 86. This is a significant number in that one of the most important *Names of God* is also numerically equal to 86. Kabbalah therefore tells us that God expresses Himself through the world around us. In other words, God is part of nature and nature is part of God.

If we want to search for God's presence, we need only look at nature, for God dwells in each area of the natural world. To damage any aspect of nature is to disconnect yourself from the Source of all sources. This is why our prayers go unanswered. We are looking to the Heavens for an invisible God instead of looking at the trees, flowers, and mountains when praying to the Creator. It is tragically ironic that we pray every day while, at the same time, we damage our connection to the very Force that we pray to.

It is only by sharing and caring for other people *and the environment* that we make contact with the Divine around us and within us. This is how our prayers are answered.

The great kabbalists of history tell us that when we look at nature or a wild creature and we realize that it is part of the Divine, part of the shattered consciousness that makes up the entire physical world, we actually elevate that creature, plant, or mountain back to its original pristine state of wholeness. In turn, we achieve a deep sense of wholeness within ourselves. Thus, if our actions are constantly in tune with this kind of whole consciousness, we can repair the world each day with our eyes, our thoughts, our deeds, our actions, and our behavior—a true holistic approach to healing. This is what will inevitably create Eden on Earth. If, however, we do not recognize the Godliness of the creatures that walk among us, the mountains that tower over us, or the atmosphere that gives us life, we will continue creating fragmentation in our world. This is why holes start appearing in the ozone layer. If our consciousness lacks wholeness, our world lacks wholeness. If there is darkness in our consciousness, there is darkness in the water, darkness in the land, darkness in the skies. Thus, the water, land, and sky cannot share with us to their full capacity.

It is human consciousness that drives the cosmos and determines its state of health.

Double-Blind Test

Science has confirmed what the ancient kabbalists revealed twenty centuries earlier. Science has repeatedly proven that consciousness creates reality. One such study—*"Can an effect precede its cause?"* by H. Schmidt— proved that consciousness can even reach back into time and affect the past.

The power and influences of consciousness have been tested and proven on so many occasions that scientists now use the double-blind test for all the experiments that they conduct. The double-blind test means that, in order for a test to be truly accurate and accepted as an authentic scientific experiment, the person doing the experiment cannot know what the test is supposed to achieve or what part of the experiment is the real test versus which part is the control. Why? The moment the individual doing the test has an expectation, his consciousness influences the outcome. In other words, the scientist and the experiment are one, on a deeper level of reality. They are both made of atoms. Thus, the scientists' brain waves influence the atoms in the experiment, for all are one on the sub-atomic level.

This confirms the kabbalistic view that, through our consciousness, we can heal our planet by virtue of how we treat others and how we view and treat our environment.

Crime and Punishment

The biblical concept of protecting trees and every part of the fabric of Creation is clearly rooted in spirituality. There are many so-called laws that appear in the Bible but these laws are rooted in the rehabilitation and elevation of one's consciousness and not a system based on revenge and retribution—despite what the literal stories tell us. When a crime against nature or man is committed, kabbalists look for a spiritual remedy as opposed to vengeance through punishment.

Traditional *punishment*, in the kabbalistic view, is akin to reprimanding a puppy for constant *accidents* on the carpet. The puppy eventually responds to the punishment.

But it's learned, robotic behavior. It's not consciousness. Likewise, punishing human beings for crimes will
in no way elevate the consciousness of the individuals
so that they inevitably recognize the underlying unity of
reality. Thus, a traditional punishment, set forth by a
court and judge, will only treat the symptom but not
remedy the underlying cause which brought about the
crime in the first place.

For instance, if someone causes any kind of damage
or injury to another individual, he or she has disrupted the natural balance of the world. The offender not
only negatively impacts the victim, but also affects all
the people who rely on the injured party as well.
Harmony is disrupted on many levels. Thus, the kabbalists point out that, in the Bible, the concept of jail
is not even mentioned in relation to any crimes committed. A person guilty of a serious crime would
appear before a Judge whose primary purpose was to
evaluate the imbalance the guilty party brought about
in the lives of the victim and the world at large, on a
spiritual and physical level. The Judge would then

strengthen his own consciousness so that he embodied the Divine Energy and Light that emanated from the Creator. The Judge would decree a suitable sentence that would help *heal* the scars and pain and, most important, *restore* the universal balance in the world. Justice was not based upon revenge or punishment but repair, healing, and transformation of the guilty party so that he or she would never commit the crime again. Not out of fear of punishment, but rather because of a new state of consciousness that recognized the unity and thus the senselessness of hurting another human or the environment. This level of consciousness thus allows the individual to contribute positive energy to the whole. Not only do such individuals replenish that which they took, they infuse even more positive energy, which helps transform the world further. When individuals truly feel the pain of injuring another human being or their environment, as if it were a limb of their own body, they would never dream of hurting anyone or anything. Thus, the goal of the justice system, according to Kabbalah, should be to raise one's consciousness so that one may perceive true reality—the oneness and interconnect-edness of everything.

If the courts and justice system merely mete out punishments to fit a crime, the cause is not being addressed. Worse, the punishment inflicts even more pain on the cosmos by damaging the offender by way of revenge. This too injects negativity and darkness into the world. Now the environment is being fed darkness from every side—the criminals, the courts, and the jails. Inevitably, the accumulation of darkness becomes so great that it spills into the environment, and that is the ultimate cause of its deterioration.

From the kabbalistic perspective, the role of the police, the lawyers, the judges, and the justice system must play a far more spiritual role than even that of the religious authority. It is this kind of consciousness that greens the world.

The Consciousness Factor

The role of consciousness is the key factor in the welfare of the environment and our personal lives. If consciousness is exposed to darkness, physically or spiritually, this affects the thoughts, behavior, and actions of the individual. The only goal must be to raise one's consciousness out of darkness and into Light. Raising consciousness is often misunderstood. It's not about being more aware of an issue or more informed. It's about purity, not the attainment of knowledge. It's about connecting to positive energy, increasing the Light and energy in one's consciousness, not acquiring more information or data.

The great 16th century Kabbalist Rav Isaac Luria said it was important for people to live in homes where they could see the blue sky from all the windows of the house. It was important for the human soul, which was nourished by the energy that permeates the sky and the light that radiates from the sun. Perhaps this is why suicide rates are higher in countries where rain, gray clouds and darkness predominate.

The kabbalists of history said it was critical for people to live in an environment where they see trees rise, flowers grow, and roses bloom. This flow of life and everyday miracles of nature creates an opening within the human soul. It illuminates one's consciousness, and this is what helps us treat others with more kindness and tolerance. There is a constant interaction and a dynamic interplay between the atoms in our brain and the atoms in our environment. Atoms are nothing more than particles of consciousness and when positive consciousness is exposed to other forms of positive consciousness they feed and nourish each other, creating something far greater and far more illuminating.

The Animal Kingdom

The great Kabbalist Rav Isaac Luria (the Ari) is considered to be one of the greatest kabbalists of history. He was gifted with the ability to see far beyond the five senses and, because of his greatness, he had chosen only a few wise students to be among his privileged group.

One day when the Ari was teaching some of the deep mysteries of the Universe, he suddenly stopped and looked up at one particular student. The Ari demanded that the student leave the room at once. When the student asked why, the Ari said that he could not be in the same room with him because the student's connection to the Divine Realm was blocked. The student was obviously shocked and began sobbing. He begged his master to explain how he had lost his connection to God. The Ari told his student that there were three chickens at the student's home. These poor chickens were not fed for three days. Their pain was so great that the student lost his connection to the Divine Realm. The Ari explained it made no difference how smart the student was, or how great a kabbalist he might be. If he could not show compassion and care for God's creatures, he could not remain connected to God. The Ari then sent the student home so that he could feed the chickens. Before he left, the Ari cautioned him to feed his livestock every morning as soon as he woke up, for animals cannot ask for food or water when they are in need. Furthermore, the Ari warned him not to blame his wife or his servants for not feeding his livestock. As owner and head of the household, it was his responsibility to ensure everyone did their job properly.

This story sheds a profound light on the importance of caring for every living creature and on our absolute accountability for all the pain in the world. More important, life is not about how smart or knowledgeable we are. It's about how compassionate and loving we are. If we measure our lives by this yardstick, we connect to the whole and find inner happiness and true serenity. This truth is exemplified in the most important event in all of the Bible.

The Power of Moses

Moses, the great leader and messenger of God, freed the Israelites from slavery after 400 years of bondage in Egypt. Moses is considered to be one of the greatest sages of human history. Yet it wasn't Moses's wisdom, humility, inner strength, or charisma that made him God's choice to deliver the Israelites from slavery.

God had chosen Moses for one singular reason—
Moses had exerted extraordinary effort to save the life
of a single lost lamb. God knew that if Moses could
demonstrate such mercy and care for a seemingly
unimportant creature like a lamb, he could be the true
Shepherd of the Israelites and thus become the chan-
nel for Revelation for all humankind. Our greatness is
measured by the amount of love and care we have for
one another. It has nothing to do with our degree of
knowledge or our accumulation of assets.

THE SINKING SHIP

The *Zohar*'s insights about our mutual responsibility for one another and the interconnectedness of all humanity is explained by way of a simple story. Once there was a massive cruise ship sailing the Atlantic Ocean. The cost for a room on board this ship was exorbitant. Nevertheless, it sold out and now the ship was far out at sea, cruising along in the middle of the night. It turns out that a passenger awoke during the night upon hearing a lot of noise coming from the cabin next to his. He climbed out of bed, put on a robe, and knocked on the door of the adjacent cabin. A man answered. He was covered in dust and perspiring. The passenger asked the man what all the commotion was. The man said he was simply drilling a hole in his cabin, which also explained why he was covered in dust. Upon hearing that rather shocking answer, the passenger looked in the room and was aghast. There was a fairly deep hole in the floor of the cabin. "Are you crazy?" the passenger screamed. "You cannot drill a hole in the cabin."

To which the man replied, "It's not your business. I paid a lot of money for my room and I can do whatever I like here."

The passenger replied, "You are mad. Don't you realize that you will sink the entire ship and kill the other passengers as well?"

Needless to say, the passenger called security and the man was arrested.

The story may sound overly simplistic but, in fact, it is life. We all believe, mistakenly, that we can do whatever we want in our life and that it has no bearing on the rest of the world. As foolish as the man in the cabin was, that is how foolish we are every day for not recognizing we are all on the same boat. We float or sink together. Kabbalistically speaking, one person's actions can sink an entire ship. Likewise, one person's actions can sink an entire world. Alternatively, one person's actions can save the entire ship and elevate the entire world. Thus our behavior, every day, at every moment, changes the world and tilts it toward destruction or healing. Each of us has that power.

The problem is we are blind to the influences that we exert on humanity and our environment. This is perhaps the biggest of all delusions. The reason we do not detect the impact we have on the globe is because every other person on Earth impacts the globe at the very same time. Thus, we cannot measure or sense the lone ripple effect of our individual actions. The state and condition of the world is merely the sum total of all human behavior and interactions. If we truly saw the implications of our deeds, we'd realize that we can, indeed, change the world by respecting and caring for our neighbors, all living creatures and each speck of matter that makes up the one planet Earth.

The Power of Green

The story of Creation in the Bible reveals how the world was created in seven days. Kabbalah explains the entire story is a code. God doesn't require a work week in order to construct a Universe. There is a simple lesson in this Genesis story that is relevant to our topic. When describing the days of Creation, specifically day one, Genesis tells us that there was a night, there was a day, and it was one day. The kabbalists point out that the word used by the Bible is not *first day* but rather *one day*. The word *first* was purposely omitted because *first* implies the concept of a second. The Bible deliberately used the word *one* instead. This implies the concept of *oneness*. Wholeness. Meaning all the days of Creation *were* unified as *one* seed in *day one*. There was a simple, all-embracing unity.

On the second day, the Bible says, everything was separated. Thus, one becomes two and the concept of *many* or *more than one* is introduced for the first time. Interestingly, the Bible does not say that the second day is good. Why? Separation is never good. Fragmentation *is* the cause of our problems. The second day is what we, as human beings, came to repair. We came to put the puzzle back together again. To restore the oneness.

On the third day of Creation, trees and vegetation were created. The color associated with the trees and vegetable kingdom is, of course, green. Kabbalistically, green is known as the color of perfect balance. It vibrates in the middle of the scale of electromagnetic waves. Green is the color that receives the rays of the sun and also shares back energy with the planet. A perfect balance of receiving and sharing. Green consciousness or *thinking green* refers to balance, wholeness, and oneness. It's about recognizing the separation and restoring the pieces to their original, indivisible state. It's about transcending one's personal needs and taking into account the needs of the whole, of which you are part. To consider the whole is to consider one's own needs. To focus on yourself is to cut yourself off from the whole and thus to deny yourself a constant flow of abundance.

Planting a Tree of Life

The great kabbalists of history had an ancient tradition: When a child was born, the parents went out to plant a tree. Why? The child is going to take from the world as he or she grows and matures. In order to restore balance, one must plant a tree to provide everything the child will need throughout life. This includes wood to build a home, fruit to eat, shade for comfort, wood for fuel to provide warmth, and oxygen so that the child will have air to breath. Furthermore, trees conserve water so the tree ensures the child will have enough water to drink. And the leaves of the tree filter the air that the child will breathe.

We can now understand why, kabbalistically, the tree is the symbol of balance and of consciousness (*Tree of Life* versus *Tree of Knowledge*). A human being is considered to be a tree of the field. Every human being is like a tree and every tree is like a human being and we are implored by the Bible to treat it as a living, breathing creature.

This profound understanding extends to the bushes and grass that surround the trees. The ancient kabbalists tell us that every expanse of grass is a melodic song, and it has a special effect on the human heart.

The Hebrew word for *bushes* also means *speech* and *words*. Thus, every bush speaks, every flower talks, and all of nature sings us a song. The trees, flowers, bushes, and blades of grass each have their own unique angels that they bring into this world, and this is why we gain so much from watering and growing flowers and nurturing trees, because it brings positive angels—spiritual energetic influences—into our environment. This is why we love gardens, the scent of flowers, and lush green meadows on a sun-soaked spring day.

The New Year for the Trees

Trees are so important that the Bible designated a calendar for the trees. Their new year is an actual holiday, or as we understand it kabbalistically, a day of connection, which occurs in the month of Aquarius on the 15th day. This is the day trees receive their spiritual nourishment for the entire year. For humans, it is an opportunity to connect to the consciousness of the trees. Trees have the ability to rise against gravity. Gravity, according to Kabbalah, is the consciousness and force that makes us take without sharing. Planting a tree and eating of its fruits on the day of the *New Year of the Trees* instills within us the power and strength to resist and rise up against our own gravitational pull— the limited consciousness that only sees the one self and not the whole. So not only do the trees help us on an environmental level, on the day of their New Year they also share with us their unique consciousness as we eat their fruits and nuts.

WATER WORLD

Ask anyone to draw you a picture and most times you will find a lake, a river, or some kind of water present in the picture. Water is our life force and it is ingrained into our very being, spiritually and physically. Our vacations and moments of tranquility almost always revolve around bodies of water. We gravitate to water every chance we get. Showers rejuvenate us. Drinking water refreshes us. There is a mystical energetic experience that takes place when we are splashing ourselves with cool, crystal-clear water. We love it hot, when steaming or soaking in a bath or spa. We love it cool, swimming in it on a hot summer's day. We love it as mist when in a desert climate. We love it as snow when in a cold climate.

However, kabbalists tell us that water is not an endless well when it comes to refreshing us, enriching us, and instilling within us simple happiness and life.

Water is the most under-appreciated resource on the planet. We take it for granted on a scale that is criminal.

Thousands of years ago, the kabbalists and biblical scholars wrote extensively on how to treat and care for water to avoid its pollution and degradation. When water is polluted with negative consciousness, all of its healing powers are lost. During the flood of Noah, the waters actually brought about destruction, a direct reflection of the destruction consciousness of humankind.

Water is crystal-clear, colorless, and odorless, which makes it able to perfectly reflect and mirror the consciousness of humankind. It assumes any shape and magically dissolves and cleanses away both physical and spiritual soil and grime. Water has been associated with immortality and eternal youth for millennia, most notably as the proverbial fountain of youth. Ancient cultures innately understood the intrinsic healing properties of this mysterious liquid.

Today, water is running scarce. Our lakes, springs, rivers, seas, which just a few decades ago were an abundant natural resource for so much nourishment and happiness, are now dying or already dead. The ecosystem is being devastated because of pollution and waste; people are taking so much from the water but they are not giving anything back to the system. There is a tragic lack of balance. When the lakes die, the springs die, and the rivers die, the whole ecosystem will be affected; a whole underwater world of creatures, animals, bacteria, and vegetation living inside every lake and every river, large and small, will die off. The water will be unable to provide for us any longer.

Longevity of Water

The Bible is filled with stories of people who lived to two or three-hundred years of age. Some lived to be more than five-hundred years old. Kabbalah reveals it was the power of the water that injected these individuals with their incredible life force and longevity. After the Flood of Noah, however, the waters became corrupted and they lost their full healing and restorative powers.

Today, kabbalistically speaking, we are at a crossroads. The water is on the verge of drying up and deteriorating into poison. By the same token, it is always darkest before the dawn. Thus, the kabbalists who lived some 500 years ago said that, when the 21st century was upon us, a shift in human consciousness would see the rejuvenation of the Earth's waters and their powerful healing properties.

That time is now. If we transform our consciousness and behavior so that we treat each part of our world with kindness and care, the waters will transform before our very eyes. This is the promise of Kabbalah.

But we must always remember: water does not belong to us. Neither does the Earth. Or the soil. Our hold on the Earth is merely a temporary lease and the lease is broken when we disrupt the balance and damage the goods.

The moment we begin treating the Earth and the people around us as a priceless natural resource, as a divine loan from God for us to interact with for the purpose of mastering green consciousness (which I will explain shortly), the Earth and our environment will mirror this transformation in human consciousness. That's when the magic of green materializes before our very eyes.

Let us now examine the magic of green and discover exactly what Gore got a few years ago. As a preface to this, allow me to share a very famous kabbalistic story.

WHO OWNS WHAT?

Many centuries ago, a wise sage was walking in the countryside when he came across two farmers engaged in a heated argument. Turns out it was the beginning of the sowing season and the two farmers were disputing the border between their respective two fields. Well, it quickly turned into quite a fiery shouting match as each farmer tried to prove that his field was the larger one and, thus, the border should be moved accordingly. The debate raged on as each offered up his own calculation and proof in order to win the argument.

The wise sage suddenly interrupted. He asked both farmers why they were arguing so intensely. Each farmer gave his side of the story, doling out the facts as to why the extra portion of the field belonged to him. With neither farmer budging from his position, they both realized that the wise sage could probably arbitrate the dispute and settle this once and for all. The sage agreed and replied, "So you are both claiming that the extra area of the field belongs to you. Tell me, did you ever think of asking the Earth which one of you it might belong to?"

They both looked at each other and shrugged. "We never thought about that," one of the farmers replied. "Is there a way to ask the Earth?"

"Of course there is", the sage replied.

"Well neither one of us knows how—can you ask the Earth on our behalf and resolve this dispute?"

"I will."

The sage then slowly kneeled down onto the field. As he did, a dry hot wind kicked up and a large ominous cloud rolled in overhead. The two farmers watched anxiously. The sage leaned down toward the Earth and began whispering ever so quietly. The wind gusted stronger. He then turned his head and put his ear against the Earth to listen to the Earth. Storm clouds suddenly filled the sky above them. The sage listened attentively. Both farmers were eager to know what was being said. The sage then slowly nodded his head in agreement to the Earth and unhurriedly stood back up. The wind picked up and began howling.

"Well, who does it belong to?" one of the Farmers asked.

"I asked the Earth that very question", replied the sage. "I asked which one of you it belongs to…This farmer or that farmer."

"And?"

A booming sound of thunder rolled across the heavens as a blast of wind kicked up a cloud of dust.

"The Earth answered, 'They both belong to me'!"

And isn't that the truth? We fight over land. We use it, abuse it, and lose it. But in the end, it is we who wind up in the Earth.

The ancient kabbalists were clear about this. Not only can we green up our world and our very own consciousness, we can transform this entire planet into a real-world Garden of Eden.

According to the teachings of the *Zohar*, Eden is not some faraway fantasy land, a mythical biblical locale that existed at the time of Creation. Eden is our future. Eden will become a practical reality once human beings transform their consciousness so that kindness, tolerance, and unconditional care become the hallmarks of human civilization. The moment that transformation occurs, the Earth will respond in kind. The *Zohar* says all the cures for all the sicknesses and diseases already exist in the plants that populate our planet. When humanity changes, these remedies will be discovered and disease will be wiped from the face of the Earth. As we change and offer unconditional friendship and love to our neighbors, the waters of the Earth will revert to their former pristine state and heal and rejuvenate the body, increasing our longevity beyond what you might dare to imagine.

This is our destiny. It is only waiting for us to find the green within before it becomes manifest. The perfect balance between giving and receiving—with our fellow humans and with our environment—is the way we transform our world into an eternal Garden of Eden where the favorite color was, and always has been, luscious *green*!

This miraculous transformation is waiting to happen—provided we get what Gore got.

Chapter Four

the origins of
trash and the
secret of Al Gore

GETTING GREEN

Gore got green for one reason and one reason only. Gore first got rid of his own garbage before telling everyone else to do the same. What is the garbage I am referring to? It isn't leftover food. It isn't nuclear waste. It isn't yesterday's newspaper, cut grass, or kitty litter.

Sit down. Brace yourself. You were hoodwinked the entire time you were reading the first chapter. You thought I was talking about normal garbage. I wasn't. You probably have no idea what kind of garbage I was referring to. But I am going to end all that right now. I am going to share with you the authentic garbage that inevitably produces the physical garbage and waste you see and observe with your five senses. The garbage I speak of is what causes all the fear, anxiety, and pain that we experience emotionally. This is the only garbage there is on Earth. Once this garbage is removed, the garbage you see all around you and feel inside of you will vanish—gently, simply, and peaceful-ly. Beyond what you would ever hope for.

The garbage is ego.

And that's what Al Gore trashed when he lost the election.

Loss of Ego

Gore took it like a man. Not an egocentric cocky man. A real man. Vulnerable. Hurting. Experiencing the raw pain of losing. Gore endured a large measure of humiliation in his defeat. In fact, he experienced the worst possible kind of defeat but also the most powerful as it relates to tossing one's ego into the trash can:

Gore was defeated, even though he was the victor, and he accepted it, for the greater good. He did grin and bear it.

Gore's Real Power

Al Gore's success, kabbalistically speaking, thus far, in his campaign against Global Warming has little to do with his PowerPoint presentation, his documentary, his status as a former vice-president and presidential candidate, or his globe-trotting lectures that try to raise the consciousness of the world. Many have tried and been less successful.

Gore's success in his fight against Global Warming is because people felt the Light and Energy that flowed through Al Gore when he removed his ego. Gore flew coach. Gore carried his own briefcase. He took on a cause from a place of true humility after the ego suffered a bruising.

Whether Gore did it on purpose or not makes no difference. When you lose your ego, you lose your *garbage*. And then there is an opening for the true self, the power of the soul, to flow through, for there is less *stuff* clogging up the pipes. People now feel his soul, his Light, and that is what motivates them into action. People, subconsciously, want what this person has. That inner Light. The deep sense of soul. Energy. The courage to embrace pain of the ego. If Gore ran again, he would have flushed something else down the toilet—all the good inner work he accomplished while out of office, which in turn affected the external work of raising the consciousness of the world on the issue of Global Warming. Ninety-nine percent of the people in this world sell out when pleasure and power come to tantalize and feed the ego. Good intentions, dreams, and ideals vanish. Gore resisted. He allowed a lifelong dream and ambition to die and, along with it, his own ego. Unfortunately, our world doesn't measure greatness by the amount of ego that dies. Our world does the opposite. We measure greatness by the amount of accomplishment an ego achieves. But in the eyes of the kabbalists, Gore achieved far more greatness than many U.S. president in history.

The kind of positive energy that truly heals the world cannot flow through a person with ego. Any individual who achieves power through ego and self-interest is using the power of negative energy to intimidate, charm, and coax people into following them or yielding to them. But in the end, chaos finds its way into the lives of both the leader and the follower. Somewhere, somehow, sooner or later, a price is paid, even if we don't connect the dots. This is the greatest secret of Kabbalah. It's a simple one, but the most difficult one to master.

Turmoil and Chaos

Ego always leads to chaos. Always. The only reason we haven't figured that out yet is because of *time*. Time is a funny thing. It plays tricks on us. Ask Einstein or any physicist what *time* actually is and they will mumble, stutter, and then scratch their heads and admit they have no idea.

Kabbalah defined *time* over twenty centuries ago. Time is the space between cause and effect. If the space is large enough, time delays the consequences of ego long enough that, when the maelstrom inevitably strikes, we view it as a random occurrence. And, just like that, we've been snowed. We think life lacks order.

The fact is, there are no random occurrences. Ever see an oak tree randomly occur full-grown on your front lawn for no apparent reason whatsoever? Didn't think so. Everything has a *seed*. Somewhere. Every turn of good fortune has a seed and so does every bit of chaos. We just call it *random* because we forgot about the seed that we alone planted so long ago. Hence, we attribute good fortune to a lucky roll of the dice. Or the dealer simply dealt us good cards because the shuffle finally went our way.

You will never get green until you realize the ego is the only garbage there is. The ego keeps us focused on symptoms and effects. The ego has us *clean* the environment instead of *cure* it.

It blinds us to the hidden causes behind our chaos. We clean our chaos but it returns later because we are addressing the effect and not the cause; we are dabbling with the branch instead of altering the DNA of the seed.

This is why most believe, mistakenly, that Gore was successful because of his PowerPoint and documentary. No one connected the dots. We were flimflammed by our own egos.

All chaos—physical and spiritual—is born of ego.

In just a bit I will tell you why it's nearly impossible for us to believe that the above statement is true. But first, let's discover what the ego really is and how one loses it, whether they like it or not, during one's life. In turn, we will see how the ego is the underlying cause of all our problems.

Defining Ego

People make the mistake of thinking ego is when we are full of ourselves and believe we are something more than we are. Yes, that is ego. But that description does not cover the complete definition. Ego has two sides. An overblown sense of self-importance is one side. Fear, low self-esteem, guilt and depression are the other side.

Two Sides of One Coin

How can two opposite sets of emotions both be categorized as ego? Simple. Both sides of the spectrum share one common denominator: it's all about *Me*!

Both ends of the spectrum are focused solely on one-self. They are two sides of one coin and the one coin is *Me*!

That is not what life is supposed to be about. Life is about focusing on and feeling the pain of others. The more one focuses on oneself, the more that pain visits us throughout our existence. The more we overcome the need to feed the me and, instead, feed and share with others, the more happiness and fulfillment comes right back to us. It's a paradox. But that's how it works. We must connect to the external whole in order to feel whole internally.

Sooner or later, we all feel pain that weakens and diminishes our ego. Sometimes it happens during midlife, sometimes in our later years, or if we are lucky, it happens when we are young. Whenever it does happen, we wind up losing something or often everything that we built. A business. A job. A position. A family. Friends. A spouse. We look back and wonder why it all disappeared.

The reason anyone loses anything is because they acquired it through self-interest. It was all about you. Even when you gave, it was still all about you.

The quicker we get the message that self-interest underlies all of our actions, the sooner fulfillment arrives for everyone.

Don't misunderstand the meaning of self-interest, this does not mean we are not supposed to be happy; there is nothing wrong with pleasure. Happiness. Joy. Those are our destiny. The only problem is we don't know how to achieve them in a lasting way.

For instance, ego only delivers temporary gratification. Inevitably, the pleasure wears off. Once it vanishes, we'll find ourselves *doubly* ravenous for more pleasure. It was one step forward, two steps back. So now we work twice as hard to fulfill our ego. If we again fill up the ego with pleasure, it will eventually evaporate and we'll be left doubly dry and twice as desirous as we were before. It's like borrowing cash from a loan shark so you can go party. The very act of partying and receiving is increasing your debt and your future misery. If you keep borrowing to experience immediate joy, the debt will soon overtake you and that's when you invite serious trouble into your life.

So the idea is not to abstain from pleasure. What we're talking about is how to become a shrewder investor in the game of life. The idea is to learn *how* to achieve fulfillment that *lasts!* Forever!

When we resist indulging the ego, and we think of others first, there is a mirror effect. The joy we give to others reflects back to us in very real, practical ways, bringing us everything that we need to make us truly happy. I am not talking in abstract terms either. When we diminish the ego, we receive physical, spiritual, emotional, and soul-level fulfillment.

Let's now find out how life provides us with the opportunities to bid adieu to the ego and thus *live* these principles.

Three Ways

According to the ancient science, wisdom, and technology of Kabbalah, there are three ways to lose the ego. We can proactively choose to eliminate it by embracing a teaching that provides genuine tools that, figuratively speaking, gently disassemble the *atoms* (consciousness) that create the ego in our brain. These same tools then reconfigure those *atoms* into brain matter that embodies unconditional love for others. In other words, our consciousness and way of thinking is transformed by the study and the application of the tools. That's the smart way to lose the ego. There are a few mild bumps along the way, but overall, it's a path filled with pleasantness.

The second way to lose the ego is when life inevitably hands you a serious setback or a deeply agonizing situation that forces you to react. If you choose not to react and you appreciate the blessings in your life while the ego undergoes pain, you are losing an aspect of your ego. If you react to the problem with even more ego, you wind up losing your ego in the third way.

The third way is the worst way. It is the physical and emotional pain and suffering experienced by the majority of the world. A loved one dies, a business dies, health deteriorates, your body suffers, your mind agonizes, your fears expand; slowly but surely, lifetime after lifetime, the ego is ripped away, despite our addiction-driven struggles to hang onto it. This is why there is chaos in the world.

Kabbalists told us long ago that ego is a temporary field of consciousness that influences and dramatically impacts the human mind. The purpose of life is to eliminate it. As the ego is steadily eradicated from our consciousness, there is an equal measure of positive, miraculous transformation in the world. As the ego expands, there is an equal measure of destructive transformation in the world.

So, in order to understand green, we must begin with the kabbalistic axiom that will lead us to the ultimate green movement.

The axiom is: the ego is the root cause of all problems, the very seed and definition of all garbage, spiritual and physical.

Let's now prove the point.

THE COLORS OF EGO

This is a book about *green* so I will use the concept of colors to share the kabbalistic insights into the dynamics of our Universe.

According to Kabbalah, the *Zohar* refers to only three colors: red, white, and green. No blue, no yellow, no teal. Only red, white, and green. Red is the color or frequency of receiving what kabbalists refer to as left column, white represents the force of sharing which is right column, and green is the balance between the two, the central column of this Universe. According to Kabbalah, these are the only forces that exist in the Universe. Sharing, receiving, and the balance of both. But the *Zohar* explains that the ego can transform both red and white into self-serving frequencies.

When we're bombastic, self-centered, indulgent, gluttonous, and miserly, we are red. As a frequency, the color red is a dominating color that draws attention to itself and absorbs light. When we are totally sharing and big-hearted, and we're giving everything away for the greater good, we are white. White contains all colors and reflects and shares all the light it receives.

Both are most often motivated by ego. Here's why, according to Kabbalah.

Red is the lowest color of the spectrum. The problem with red is that it's all about *me*. You take. You receive. You hoard. It doesn't take long before red turns into a black hole. This means even the Light around you gets sucked into your empty void and, thus, you never find happiness.

The problem with white is that it's the same ego—*but in reverse!* You are a do-gooder. You're righteous. Moral. You give everything away. You have the right intentions. You constantly share. But you lack any red. Red is receiving. Without any aspect of healthy receiving you cannot replenish that which you gave away.

The inevitable result? You wind up giving away the entire farm. You become depleted. Empty. Depressed. Physically. And emotionally. Now you are unhappy—even if you deny it. This is why the road to hell is paved with good intentions. Sooner or later you get sick and tired of being empty after all of the giving that you did and you quickly fall into red. You start taking and grabbing because your appetite is now voracious. Which soon leads to the black hole. Or you become a victim, the deepest red there is.

When Sharing is Not Sharing

For those of you upset by the notion that constant giving without any receiving is a form of ego, your white just turned into red, thus proving my point. You are upset that you are not receiving recognition for all your giving. Thus, your giving had a hidden agenda and it cannot be defined as pure giving. True giving never elicits a response. You're totally secure, serene, and contented regardless what someone else says (or writes).

Let me clarify: I am not saying there is no such thing as pure giving. In fact, I am not saying anything at all about giving. I have no opinion on the matter. I am just sharing what the ancient kabbalists revealed in the *Zohar* some 20 centuries ago.

What they are telling us is this: there are *two* kinds of sharing. One is when we share with a subconscious hidden agenda to receive something in return. This is white, cloaking red. They also explain that there *is* a consciousness and behavioral action that is known as unconditional, pure giving, where everyone wins, where abundance is the result—for the receiver *and* the giver.

But to know how that one works, one needs to know how the Universe works.

Locating the Source

There is an infinite energy Source that underlies all physical reality that Kabbalah calls *The Light*. Most people call it God. Others refer to it as the Creator. George Lucas called it the Force. The designation is not what's important right now. What is important is the nature and substance of this Divine Force.

Our tendency has always been to look toward the sky, or the stars, or high up on a mountain for the ultimate Source of the Divine. Wrong direction, my friends. It's inside of us. Literally. Not metaphorically.

Beneath the molecules, atoms, protons, electrons, neutrons, deep beyond the leptons, quarks, bosons, and gluons, at the very fundamental level of our own physical being lies an infinite sea of luminous Energy filled with an incalculable sum of knowledge and an immeasurable, endless array of happiness, fulfillment, and joy. It's one Force. Not two. And all the knowledge and happiness that I speak of are unified as one. In other words, true happiness includes infinite knowledge and true knowledge includes infinite happiness. Please make note of the word *true*. False knowledge and false happiness are not included in this vast sea of luminous Energy. False happiness is the kind that eventually ends. If it ends, it cannot be happiness, by the true definition of the word. True happiness means *forever*. Thus, most of us have not found true happiness.

This shining, gleaming Force of Energy is the fountain and source of everything. And I do mean everything. So it's silly to say "it also includes." Everything means *everything*. Period. When you write a book, the content already existed within this Force. When you compose a song, think up a new idea, feel happy, enjoy a cheesecake, appreciate your family, all these good feelings derive from this infinite ocean of Energy. The only thing not present is the opposite of happiness. There is no pain, death, sadness, or any other feature of existence that subtracts from simple human joy.

Turns out life is not that complicated. Life only becomes complicated, painful and chaotic when we somehow disconnect ourselves from this unending Source that lies beneath the surface of existence. Do you know how we disconnect? Ego. No other reason.

The Problem with White

That being said, the nature and will of this Light or Force is to fulfill every single creature on Earth with every conceivable variety of happiness imaginable. Really!

Therein lies the problem with white. If you only give and never receive, then you are denying the very will of the Divine Energy which seeks to impart an inexhaustible flow of happiness to you. Hence, *receiving* must always be present in life.

To explain this further will only lessen the point. Thus, the question becomes: if red is all about receiving and it leads to a black hole, and if non-stop sharing (white) leads us to emptiness with a U-turn back into red, where then lies the middle ground? How do we share and still connect to the Light so that Light can give us everything, thus allowing us to share some more?

Meet the color green.

Chapter Five

green, greed, & generosity

THE POWER OF GREEN

There's a reason the Earth is green. Green occupies the middle point of the color spectrum. It embodies life and perfect balance, expressed elegantly through photosynthesis.

Green is also the essence of all spiritual life. We receive. *And* we share. A perfect balance. Total receiving is red. Total sharing is white. Receiving fused with sharing in the right balance is the power of green, according to Kabbalah.

But there exists another vital and critical element. Pay attention: The intent and conscious thought *behind* sharing and receiving must be *flipped* inside out as I will shortly explain. Let's call this *inside-out* action The Flip.

The Flip is the key to everything. And you should know that it can take a lifetime to master it. But as you develop it, life only continues to get better.

We now know, based on our kabbalistic axiom, that in this dimension of reality ego motivates both red and white. Receiving (red) leads to chaos and sharing (white) without receiving leads to chaos.

There is only one formula that leaves ego out of the question and thus eliminates chaos from our life—The Flip!

The Green Formula—The Art of The Flip

When we share, it must be for one singular purpose: *to receive energy*. Not a monetary reward. Not praise, honor, acclaim, or feelings of self-righteousness. Our sole objective is to receive energy that will diminish our ego. The act of sharing is for our own self. We are not helping others or doing anyone any favors. We cannot change the world. We can only change ourselves. And *that* is what changes the world. That is the green formula. That's The Flip. Did you miss it? If so, I will elaborate.

When you give to someone else, you are really giving to yourself. *Only* to *yourself*. You are giving zero to the other person—*until* you realize that you really gave to yourself. Then another Flip occurs. The person you gave to now *receives* something from you after all.

I know. It's a bit tricky. Work with me.

Mastering The Flip

How does sharing help you specifically?

You can call it spiritual energy or a metaphysical influence or just plain old Light. Some call it the Hand of God. Whatever you choose to call it, this invisible Force of Energy is suddenly aroused from the *sub*-subatomic realm where the ocean of Infinite Energy dwells each time you share with the consciousness that you alone are benefiting. You summon this energy and Light when you do an act of *unconditional* sharing and use The Flip. Unconditional means we do not derive or expect any material or ego-pleasing reward or payment. *What* we seek to receive, exclusively, is the Light we ignite in the unseen realm of Divine Energy.

Here's why:

We use this Light to diminish darkness within us. All darkness—be it fear, insecurity, the need for approval, the need to feel superior—these are all just different aspects of one phenomenon—*ego*! As darkness (and ego, the cause of darkness) begin to disappear from our being, we grow happier and more fulfilled. And that feels a whole lot better than false praise from people who don't really care about us.

So, in your mind, when you share with anyone, you must realize that you are receiving and that what you seek is a mysterious energy force that will wipe out a portion of your ego, because the ego is what causes all your pain and all the pain in this world. When that energy force removes a measure of ego, suddenly you feel fulfillment.

The problem is that ninety-nine percent of the world has never felt that deep fulfillment that I am talking about. I didn't say people do not feel fulfillment in general. I am saying when you reach inside and take in a wave of Light from the ocean of Infinite Energy, it's the kind of fulfillment that is as addictive and pleasurable as cocaine, heroin, or a single malt scotch—in a positive spiritual kind of way, of course. But it's only available relative to the amount of ego that you lose and genuine kindness that you evolve. It takes a lifetime to reach that ocean inside. But when you do, you are now motivated to transform yourself out of pure greed. You want that energy. You crave those feelings. So you share with others because you know deep in your gut, deep in places where you never thought blissful pleasure could reach, that it is *you*, and only *you* who are benefiting by your loving, caring, unconditional pure acts of kindness. But before your true greed evolves, there is a temporary process where ego-eradication is a bit painful.

That is the pain Gore endured. He took it. Nothing more. And thus, all of his subsequent physical actions were filled with the Light that Gore summoned on the night he conceded the election.

This leads us to a very important question. Why is The Flip so hard to do? Why do ninety-nine percent of us run the opposite direction when our egos are dented?

AN OLD SECRET FINALLY REVEALED

Want to know a really, really old secret about the true nature of reality? The entire world, all of humankind, is connected—on a quantum level—to a single Negative Force that creates and sustains the ego in everyone. Kabbalah calls this Negative Force *The Adversary*. The essential nature of this Negative Force is *doubt*. Therefore, by virtue of being inside of you, it impels you to doubt and disbelieve in its very existence. See the paradox?

The closer you get to this Negative Force, the greater the doubt you feel because doubt emanates from its very presence. This is how it survives.

The term *Adversary* was given to this force because it describes its purpose and function in this physical reality. To act as an adversary means *to oppose*, to challenge.

Essentially, the adversarial force pushes and propels you away from truth. It is the adversarial force we strive against in the game of life. This is why it is so hard to find real truth and live it. For instance, the truth is, we *should* eat healthy. But the adversarial force pushes us—against our will—toward eating everything we know we shouldn't.

Exercise and physical fitness are good for us. That is truth. The adversarial force impels us to be lazy, inactive, and lethargic. Those influences *are* the Adversary in full expression.

Recreational narcotics and prescription meds are dangerous. That is a truth. The addiction they cause *is* the expression of the adversarial force.

This negative force is imbedded into every cell of our body and it is the root behind all addiction. More precisely, addiction is just another name for the adversarial force. Get it? The ancient Kabbalah and modern-day medical science are simply using two distinct terms to describe one single phenomenon. The only difference between Kabbalah and medical science is that Kabbalah ascribes consciousness and purpose to this counterforce. In other words, it's there for a reason. It's not purposeless, random, or an accident of the Universe. Those kinds of notions are simply the Adversary in action—pulling you away from the truth.

Why does this adversarial force exist? And how does one find it if it has the power to envelop us with skepticism, doubt, darkness, and total disbelief? I will answer the latter question first, and then we can proceed to the first question.

How to Identify and Recognize the Adversarial Force
The very moment you make the effort to just fight it, you've won the first round. As a result, *truth* will filter into your consciousness. Remember, the proof must be in the pudding. But make no mistake—the first step is the hardest one to make. You must overcome a mountain of doubt, all your belief systems, and just be open—only for a second—to the possibility that it *does*

exist. Not metaphorically, not as some natural phenomenon of the human body or as the Second Law of
Thermodynamics, but a real conscious force oozing
with purpose.

Do that now. Just for a moment. Let go. Trust it. Try it.
If you let go, and you don't feel a glimmer—or an ava-
lanche—of truth filling your being, you've lost nothing.
If you do feel truth, you are on your way to getting
green. Why? This is the force that impels us to be either
red or white. In other words, our ego causes us to be
self-centered—red—expressed through our constant
taking and receiving. Self-indulgent receiving can
range from mild selfishness to extreme, insatiable,
megalomaniacal greed.

Likewise, this force impels us to constantly give, which
is white. This includes simple acts of sharing with others because we want to be loved or we're afraid to say
no. In this case we are sharing to *receive* approval.
Thus, white is merely being used as a camouflage to
conceal red. In a more excessive case, our giving is

fueled by a sanctimonious, self-righteous, holier-than-thou state of consciousness.

In both situations we're unaware of the ego's hidden agenda.

Green Shines a Light

The only time we find a middle ground is when we stop—just for a moment—to consider the motive behind our behavior. This action of *stopping* is how one gets green. We must use the color green to shine a light on a force that has been largely undetected for over 20 centuries.

So once again, I ask you. Take a moment and admit to yourself there is a hidden agenda behind all your actions. Consider the real possibility that the adversarial force is as authentic as the unseen atoms in the air. It's a no-lose proposition. It will only hurt your ego if you try it (which is precisely the point).

You're not going to scrape your elbow or contract the flu or come down with pneumonia simply because you made a slight shift in your consciousness. Now do you see why the first step is the most difficult? It's so easy, it's so darn simple, this force *must* fabricate the greatest illusion of all—its non-existence. So this conscious and very shrewd adversarial force will now attempt to make you feel foolish. Or silly. Or skeptical. Or perhaps you're feeling intellectually superior to the author and this whole exercise is simply beneath you.

I think Andre Gide, the Nobel Prize-winning French author, put it best. Gide says one must have a *belief* in God in order to serve God, but one does not need a belief in the devil in order to serve him.

Replace the word *devil* with *the Adversary* and then use your free will to engage in the exercise or pass it up.

THE PROBLEM WITH ACTIVISM

Al Gore was not being an activist. Al Gore transformed himself, relatively speaking, into an agent of change. But the change was *internal*. It happened in his consciousness the moment he stood in front of a nation and conceded defeat. In that one singular moment, the PowerPoint, the documentary, and his entire effort to thwart Global Warming was seeded, nurtured, and transformed into a full-fledged tree with a Nobel Prize and an Oscar dangling from its branches instead of peaches or plums. It all happened right there. That night. As his ego took a beating. Why didn't he know it at the time? If he could have somehow seen the future, Gore would have lost his free will. If he knew *ahead of time* the good that would transpire by taking a thumping of the ego, then the diminishing of ego could never have taken place. It's illogical. There would be a measure of self-interest. Gore would see the payoff in advance. And that's a problem. It's a paradox. Why? The ego is all about self-interest. Therefore you cannot defeat the ego if self-interest is present because self-interest *feeds* the ego.

It's Never Intellectual

Becoming more intellectually aware of a problem is not how one raises consciousness. Everyone thinks awareness is consciousness-raising—but it's not, according to Kabbalah. Consciousness-raising is when we identify the ego and Adversary as genuine distinct forces, separate from our true self. If you are not aware of your true self (you and the adversarial force) how can you possibly evolve awareness for the rest of the world?

The adversarial force will even hand us the correct information about an issue, the correct physical solution provided we grasp it through our ego and apply it under the guise of sharing. Under that scenario, we are cleaning our world—not greening it. A dangerous but clever ploy on the part of the adversarial force. Think about it, we can all be busy driving "green" cars and protecting the environment from harmful, toxic emissions, but if we allow ourselves to get angry and cheat our neighbor, then as we drive proudly to work feeling good about our contribution to "clean" the environment, our anger will cause a volcano to erupt in Alaska that will do more damage to the environment than the combined emissions of all the cars in North America.

Internal Versus External

Activists want to change the world. But most don't want to change themselves. When I refer to activists I am referring to me. And you. We are *all* activists when you get right down to it. Activist means you try to change others. That's it. Nothing more. And it's futile. It's cleaning. Not greening.

The problem is, no one recognizes the ego inside the activist within all of us. And that's okay, for now. But it's not okay forever. In other words, it's an innate human trait to want to teach and change others. That is merely the adversarial force pushing us in the wrong direction—away from our own ego. But sooner or later, all of us must come to the realization that we only change others by changing ourselves *first*. This takes a lifetime to understand. Some of us might believe or accept this premise on an intellectual level, but to truly make it your living, breathing state of consciousness, well, that's a whole other matter.

By its very definition, activism suggests an outward, external effort to change someone or something. Here's the problem with it. If you argue, fight, combat, clash, and protest against those you disagree with, then *ego* is being fed. Plain and simple. Being right or wrong has *nothing* to do with it. Right and wrong are relative concepts. Right and wrong cause wars and wars breed genocide. Being right doesn't allow one to disrespect another human being in the name of rightness. That is just dumping your garbage on the person you oppose. Your enemy now retaliates and he dumps his garbage on you. It is the ego being fed on both sides of the battle lines. The ego wins and humankind loses. The ego is the garbage that will consume our planet unless we kill it.

When you eradicate your own ego, you help weaken and diminish the ego in your enemy, which now gives your enemy a fighting chance to finish off the rest of his or her ego. If you argue, you only feed the ego of the enemy and, thus, you are creating the very monster that is coming after you.

Turns out we have been playing the game of life *backwards*. We've been living in red and white instead of green. Thus, the spilling of red and white blood cells has been the trademark of humanity for countless centuries.

If you love your children, your spouse, your partner and your friends, you'd kill your ego fast. Why? Each time you diminish your ego, you help diminish the other person's ego. We need each other.

Let us now examine why this Universe, according to Kabbalah, came into existence with the adversarial force as part of the laws of nature and human nature.

WHY THE ADVERSARY BOTHERS TO EXIST

Free will. That's it. Nothing more than that. By pulling us away from truth, presenting us with lies instead, each human being has to work at finding the truth. Instead of paradise and truth being handed over to humans carte blanche, the effort we exert to find the real truth allows us to earn it and thus appreciate it once it becomes ours.

Life is simple.

It is the adversarial force that makes life complicated and increasingly disordered. It pushes us away from perfection and truth, hurling us toward increasing chaos and falsehood.

Chapter Six

giving & receiving
...and giving!

THE GOOD OF GREED

Free will—which consists of choosing between lies and truth—is what makes us appreciate the truth and happiness when we receive it.

Kabbalistically, we are still stuck in a world of lies. Cleaning up the Earth is a lie. It will not change the Earth. It will only displace the problem because we are not addressing the true garbage. Self-interest. Greed. Unkind behavior toward others. The lie we keep telling ourselves and believing is that there is no ego. No adversarial force keeping us in the dark. We've lived this lie for countless centuries.

Keep in mind, there is nothing wrong with greed. It's just that we are fueled by the wrong kind of greed. We choose *foolish greed* that delivers temporary pleasure at the expense of long-term chaos. That's the kind of greed that engenders non-stop receiving, self-indulgence, and ultimately destroys our environment.

There is another kind of greed that my father, Rav Berg, learned from his teacher, and he shared it with me. I like to include it in most of the books I write, so I can share it with you. It is *Enlightened Greed*. This is far more powerful and greedier than foolish greed. Enlightened Greed is what motivates us to share, care, love, and give, while at the same time wanting to receive *true* happiness—not lies and false happiness—as a result of our effort. True happiness is admitting to (and then losing) the ego because we know it's the root of our pain. We think the ego will make us happy. It won't. If we knew that, we'd work hard at losing it.

Defining Pure Giving

The kabbalists tell us that when we know, with the utmost certainty, that only we are benefiting from our sharing action, that is considered to be a pure act of giving. Now follow this carefully: *that alone is what causes the giving action to deliver true positive results.*

Those results will now strike at the seed of the physical problem because the giver addressed the true seed of the spiritual problem—his or her own egocentric self. That was The Flip. The individual shared to help himself. And it's *that* consciousness that winds up helping the other person. Once again, Gore did just that. Not on purpose. I don't think Gore was hoping to lose the election on purpose while he was campaigning across the country just so that he could build a PowerPoint instead of holding policy meetings in the Oval Office. History and destiny (I prefer Karma) decided that.

Gore's only free will was to choose between using his ego to save face or losing his ego to save the planet.

When it's Not Real Giving

When we give and we feel and believe we are helping the receiving party, everyone loses. This is called cleaning. Not greening. Cleaning is an effect that deals with the problem once it manifests. Sharing individuals give and think that their physical act is the solution. Likewise, the receiving parties feel their act of receiving is helping to solve the problem. There was no Flip. So how do we make The Flip so that we can green instead of clean?

The *Giving* Litmus Test

The litmus test for the giver is this: when you give, can you now admit, openly, in front of others, that you are deriving egocentric pleasure and that you have selfishness attached to your action? If you can admit it, you just dealt a great and powerful blow to the ego. In response, your act of giving will now launch a great and powerful blow upon the physical problem. Just don't fall into the illusion that has held us prisoner since life began: that it was the physical action that generated the result. The physical action is the apple on the branch. Your admission of ego is the apple seed planted in the dirt.

If you cannot admit, for whatever reason, that you have ego, then your giving is considered white. Not green. If you cannot look deep inside to find some kind of fault, then you are buying into the lies that the adversarial force is implanting in you, and you have not looked deep enough.

Green means you always—no matter what—look within yourself and find some aspect of selfishness, self-righteousness, preachy self-contented feelings derived from your action, to thus ensure the giving was pure. If you cannot find it, you're in denial.

But if you really care about others and, more importantly, your own inner self, then know that the very act of admitting it, to yourself and, most importantly, to others, *is* the pain (Light) that weakens and eradicates the ego. It will hurt for a moment. But then everyone around you will soon feel your Light. And with your ego weakened, there MUST be an equal measure of fulfillment flowing into your life. If it didn't work, the kabbalists would have been the most selfish, self-indulgent gluttons on the planet. My father, Rav Berg, always said kabbalists are greedy. Make no mistake about it. They don't settle for less. Instead of temporary, immediate gratification of the ego, they choose the wiser investment of long-term fulfillment that never expires.

How do you know when there is no more ego inside of you and that your sharing actions are genuine? Simple. You yourself and the world around you start to change in positive ways.

Making it Work

What is required to make this thought process and consciousness work successfully is your realization that your ego is the sole contributor to the problems you see in the world and the problems you might be experiencing in your own life. No human being on Earth will ever willingly undergo the pain associated with the gradual elimination of one's ego if they cannot perceive the true benefit. This is not about morals. It's about greed, as we're starting to figure out.

Don't Even Think About It

Before we examine the art of receiving with green consciousness, keep this forever in your mind: you cannot, and will not, be able to remove someone else's ego. That is a trap. It is the ego that impels you to try and destroy another person's ego for his or her own good.

This only serves to strengthen both your egos. It's a vicious cycle. It pollutes your being and, thus, the pollution of the world is the inevitable effect. Look around. Observe the state of the world. Did it work?

The Art of Receiving

Once you understand—and I mean truly understand—how sharing only benefits you, and when you experience and taste heartily the joy that this kind of green consciousness delivers, you will automatically know that when you are on the receiving end of a gift, you are actually *sharing* with the giver. Once again, Kabbalah just turned receiving upside down. That's The Flip that happens when you receive. You are actually sharing and you are focused on the rewards the other person is going to get in life because you tasted those rewards when you mastered the art of giving through green consciousness.

To summarize: We share out of pure, unadulterated greed. And we receive and darn well enjoy it because it's imparting *life* to the person who shared. We enjoy it for them, not for ourselves. And that way we get to enjoy it in a fashion that leaves ego out of the equation. The Flip is what sidesteps the ego.

Isn't green an interesting and funky kind of color when you stop and think about it? Green has both *greed* and *generosity* attached to it. But it's in reverse. It's like we're living in a looking-glass straight out of Alice in Wonderland.

Think about it. You share out of greed not because you are righteous. You receive because you are being generous, for you know your receiving is imparting life to the giver. Truly profound. He or she needs you as much as you need them. Perfect balance. The power of green.

It's Not the Act, It's the Consciousness

Clearly, Kabbalah does not suggest that we do not clean up the mess we've created, or that recycling our physical garbage is a waste of time. There is a very subtle and fine line that the reader must get if the reader hopes to get green.

If we recycle our garbage, write a letter to Congress, talk with others about the issue of global warming, or take any action that reduces carbon emissions in the atmosphere, and we think we are helping to clean up the world, then we are. We are *cleaning* up the world instead of greening up the world.

Now flash back. Do The Flip. Repeat the same actions I have just mentioned.

This time, *just* change the consciousness and intent behind the action. If we recycle our garbage but we realize our own ego *contributed* to it, we are turning green. Not with envy, but in state of consciousness. You see, when we use our ego in a nasty way toward friends, family, and our foes, we do create garbage in the metaphysical, spiritual arena, which is the cause-level of our physical world. I know, that is a bit abstract. Nonetheless, this is how it works. So someone screaming at their spouse in Peoria, Illinois, is polluting existence in the same way as a company that dumps toxic waste. And the fact that we do not believe this to be true is why the world continues to bleed, burn, heat up, and wallow in noxious waste.

So write a letter to Congress. We must write the letter. Get involved. We must get involved. Raise the consciousness of the world about Global Warming; change your lifestyle so that you do not physically contribute to increased pollution and the warming of the planet. But do it with *yourself* in mind. Take responsibility, blame no one else. Don't think that it is your physical act that is solving anything. Instead it is the responsibility that you are taking, it is the act of sharing that you are doing, it is the ego that you are finding in your action. Own up to the fact that when we blame business and industry for ruining our world, it makes *us* feel better about ourselves on a subconscious level. If, on the other hand, you realize that you, on a consciousness and ego level, are *one* with all the businesses and industry that pollute, you are helping to green up yourself and, in turn, the world. It's all about The Flip. It is all about the consciousness that drives our actions.

The Consciousness of Accountabllity

What Kabbalah is really saying is the only Flip we need to make is the one called *accountability*. When we see someone do something wrong, we are also accountable for their actions. Period. I know. Sounds like new age, spiritual psychobabble. It's not. It's physics.

If your finger accidentally touches a hot stove, what's the point in blaming your finger? Your legs, body, and mind also contributed to the situation. And isn't it the entire body that experiences pain and discomfort along with the finger? The finger just bears the brunt of it. Scolding your finger for the mistake is illogical.

We don't realize that we are all interconnected as one. Face it. We just don't. We have no idea what that means. First, I accept the notion that there is no blaming others—because there are no *others*.

There is only us. Humanity. And we are accountable to each other, to truly care for each other. Not just in the physical reality but, more importantly, on the level of consciousness and behavior.

THE PROMISE

If we live life like this, turning from red to green, from white to green, step-by-step, the kabbalists absolutely guarantee us that our Earth, human existence, this awesome, magnificent Divinely inspired game of life will transcend the sum of its parts. The results will be miraculous. Beyond what I am able to write on a page. And we'll get there in a manner that is ridiculously simple and joyful. And we'll scratch our heads wondering why something so simple took so long to figure out.

When our consciousness shifts from the red and white into the glorious, perfectly balanced green, all of our interrelationships with one another in business, socially, in art and entertainment, in every activity of human endeavor, will become perfect. Absolutely perfect.

The Good News

What excites me personally is that, though we are now knee-deep in the cesspool, on the verge of global devastation, we can turn it all around on a dime.

We just need to do The Flip. In our consciousness. When we do it there, it's already done. So do it now.

The moment we start practicing this in our day-to-day lives, the physical process immediately becomes filled with joy. Because, a few moments later, we suck up a wave from the infinite ocean of Divine Light and it feels good. Feels real nice. Feels like a distant memory of something that was once indescribably euphoric.

When we choose the pain proactively, in dealing with others, humbling ourselves and thinking about them first, only the ego takes a hit. But that kind of pain doesn't last long. Ask Al Gore. Ask him now if it was worth the pain he experienced the night he conceded the election, if the pain he went through winds up stopping Global Warming.

The absolute moment we decide to make a change from self-interest to selfless behavior, we start drawing the sweet-scented healing waters from the ocean of Infinite Energy. We begin experiencing those feelings of joy. Each day becomes another victory. And another. And when that final trace of self-centeredness is removed from our hearts, we win the championship. This is the ultimate path of Kabbalah and the destiny of humanity, to bring about the complete happiness and perfection of our world. It is a simple path but not always an easy one. If something I have said in this book has inspired you and awakened your mind to the true meaning of green and the work that is involved for each and every one of us in restoring our world to its purpose and color, then I invite you to look into Living Kabbalah System. This is a unique program that helps you to integrate all the tools of Kabbalah into your life every day. It guides you to really find your ego and the many ways that it shows up in your life and damages our world, while at the same time revealing to you the infinite opportunities to care for others and be a custodian of the Earth. I know of no better way to take our world back.

FULL CONTROL

We never really knew or believed that we had total control over our lives. We thought others controlled our destiny and our states of happiness. In a way, they did, because we handed over that control by virtue of living self-centered lives, living in the red and white zones instead of green.

It's an infinitely empowering notion that all of that happiness we desire and all the answers to our dreams are within us. What a hiding place! *Happiness* chose to make the game of life challenging.

Each moment we resist intolerance and embrace a little ego pain, we literally, totally make contact—not with a divine spark—but rather with an unending sea of luminous energy and Divine consciousness. When we tap into this consciousness we have the power to think a new world into existence.

If we live under self-interest, we disconnect and we wind up settling for momentary sparks of pleasure that are snuffed out in a flash. This is why our appetite for fulfillment and happiness is never satiated.

The unending well of happiness was inside of us the whole time. It's now time to tap it, suck up the waves and water of our Earth so that the healing begins now and paradise awaits, just around the corner.

It's time. For green has arrived.

Rebooting: Defeating Depression with the Power of Kabbalah

An estimated 18 million people in the United States suffer from depression—that's almost 10% of the population. So chances are good that you have, or someone you know has, been affected by it. Antidepressants, counseling, herbal remedies—all have been known to help treat the symptoms, but sometimes they fall short. If only you could click on the "Restart" button and get your internal software back on track. Now, in *Rebooting*, noted kabbalistic scholar and author Yehuda Berg shows how you can do just that by reconnecting with desire and light to emerge from this debilitating darkness.

Living Kabbalah: A Practical System for Making the Power Work for You

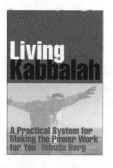

Living Kabbalah is a unique system of technology meant for you to use to transform your life and achieve true and lasting fulfillment. In these pages, you will find practical tools and exercises to help you break negative patterns, overcome challenges, and incorporate the time-tested wisdom of Kabbalah into your daily life. Noted author and teacher Yehuda Berg provides a clear blueprint that guides you step-by-step along the path toward the ultimate attainment of all that you need and desire.

Tap into a greater power—the power of Kabbalah—and learn to live more fully, richly, and joyfully every day, starting today!

THE TECHNOLOGY FOR THE SOUL™ SERIES

Beyond Blame: A Full-Responsibility Approach to Life

If you think that chaos and suffering in your life is random or caused by external circumstances, think again! It's time to take personal responsibility for life's problems rather than give in to the tendency to blame others for them. In this book, you'll find simple, practical tools to help you overcome this negative tendency and live a happier, more productive life. Learn how to eliminate "victim consciousness" and improve your life, starting today.

The Monster is Real: How to Face Your Fears and Eliminate Them Forever

Admit it—at this very moment, you're afraid of something, or maybe even lots of things. This book shows you how to attack and defeat your fears at their most basic level. It offers practical kabbalistic tools for eliminating fear at its source so you can begin to live life to its fullest extent.

The Dreams Book: Finding Your Way in the Dark

Lift the curtain of reality and discover the secrets of dream interpretation that have remained hidden for centuries. Learn powerful techniques to attract soul mates, improve relationships, recognize career opportunities, and much more. This book holds the key to navigating the dreamscape, where the answers to life's questions are revealed.

God Does Not Create Miracles, You Do!

Stop waiting for a miracle and start making miracles happen! Discover powerful tools to help you break free of whatever is standing between you and the complete happiness you deserve. This book gives you the formula for creating the connection with the true source of miracles that lies only within yourself.

Kabbalah on Love

This charming little book has a simple yet profound message: Love is not something you learn or acquire but an essence within, waiting to be revealed. Buried by layers of ego, fear, shame, doubt, low self-esteem, and other limitations, the incredibly powerful force that is love can only be activated by sharing and serving unconditionally. Only then will the layers fall away and the essence of love reveal itself. The book draws the distinction between love and need, which is a selfish product of ego, and reminds us that we cannot love someone else until we figure out how to love ourselves and connect with the love within.

The Red String Book: The Power of Protection

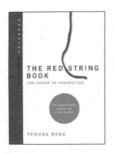

Discover the ancient wisdom behind the popularity of the Red String—the timeless technology known as Kabbalah. Worn on the left wrist, an authentic Red String provides protection against the "Evil Eye"—all negative effects that exist in the world. In *The Red String Book*, Yehuda Berg reveals how everyone can learn to use this simple yet effective tool for self-defense and healing.

Kabbalah on Pain: How to Use It to Lose It

Learn how to use your emotional pain to your advantage and how to release its grip on you forever. When you avoid, ignore, or bury your pain, you only prolong psychic agony. But Kabbalah teaches a method for detaching from the source of this pain—human ego—and thereby forcing ego to take on and deal with your pain. When you choose the path of the soul where only ego suffers, you will begin to move toward the state of pure joy that is your destiny.

The Power of Kabbalah

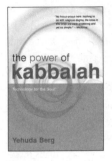

Imagine your life filled with unending joy, purpose, and contentment. Imagine your days infused with pure insight and energy. This is *The Power of Kabbalah*. It is the path from the momentary pleasure that most of us settle for, to the lasting fulfillment that is yours to claim. Your deepest desires are waiting to be realized. Find out how, in this basic introduction to the ancient wisdom of Kabbalah.

Also available: *The Power of Kabbalah Card Deck*

MORE PRODUCTS THAT CAN HELP YOU BRING THE WISDOM OF KABBALAH INTO YOUR LIFE

The Secret: Unlocking the Source of Joy & Fulfillment By Michael Berg

The Secret reveals the essence of life in its most concise and powerful form. Several years before the latest "Secret" phenomenon, Michael Berg shared the amazing truths of the world's oldest spiritual wisdom in this book. In it, he has pieced together an ancient puzzle to show that our common understanding of life's purpose is actually backwards, and that anything less than complete joy and fulfillment can be changed by correcting this misperception.

God Wears Lipstick: Kabbalah for Women
By Karen Berg

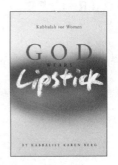

For thousands of years, women were banned from studying Kabbalah, the ancient source of wisdom that explains who we are and what our purpose is in this universe. Karen Berg changed that. She opened the doors of The Kabbalah Centre to all who would seek to learn.

In *God Wears Lipstick*, Karen Berg shares the wisdom of Kabbalah, especially as it affects you and your relationships. She reveals a woman's special place in the Universe and why women have a spiritual advantage over men. She explains how to find your soul mate and your purpose in life, and empowers you to become a better human being.

Also available: God Wears Lipstick Card Deck

Secrets of the Zohar: Stories and Meditations to Awaken the Heart
By Michael Berg

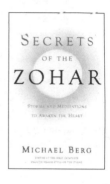

The *Zohar*'s secrets are the secrets of the Bible, passed on as oral tradition and then recorded as a sacred text that remained hidden for thousands of years. They have never been revealed quite as they are here in these pages, which decipher the codes behind the best stories of the ancient sages and offer a special meditation for each one. Entire portions of the *Zohar* are presented, with the Aramaic and its English translation in side-by-side columns. This allows you to scan and to read aloud so that you can draw on the *Zohar*'s full energy and achieve spiritual transformation. Open this book and open your heart to the Light of the *Zohar*!

Immortality: The Inevitability of Eternal Life
By Rav Berg

This book will totally change the way in which you perceive the world, if you simply approach its contents with an open mind and an open heart.

Most people have it backwards, dreading and battling what they see as the inevitability of aging and death. But, according to the great Kabbalist Rav Berg and the ancient wisdom of Kabbalah, it is eternal life that is inevitable.

With a radical shift in our cosmic awareness and the transformation of the collective consciousness that will follow, we can bring about the demise of the death force once and for all—in this "lifetime."

THE ZOHAR

Composed more than 2,000 years ago, the *Zohar* is a set of 23 books, a commentary on biblical and spiritual matters in the form of conversations among spiritual masters. But to describe the *Zohar* only in physical terms is greatly misleading. In truth, the *Zohar* is nothing less than a powerful tool for achieving the most important purposes of our lives. It was given to all humankind by the Creator to bring us protection, to connect us with the Creator's Light, and ultimately to fulfill our birthright of true spiritual transformation.

More than eighty years ago, when The Kabbalah Centre was founded, the *Zohar* had virtually disappeared from the world. Few people in the general population had ever heard of it. Whoever sought to read it—in any country, in any language, at any price—faced a long and futile search.

Today all this has changed. Through the work of The Kabbalah Centre and the editorial efforts of Michael Berg, the *Zohar* is now being brought to the world, not only in the original Aramaic language but also in English. The new English *Zohar* provides everything for connecting to this sacred text on all levels: the original Aramaic text for scanning; an English translation; and clear, concise commentary for study and learning.

THE KABBALAH CENTRE

The International Leader in the Education of Kabbalah

Since its founding, The Kabbalah Centre has had a single mission: to improve and transform people's lives by bringing the power and wisdom of Kabbalah to all who wish to partake of it.

Through the lifelong efforts of Kabbalists Rav and Karen Berg, and the great spiritual lineage of which they are a part, an astonishing 3.5 million people around the world have already been touched by the powerful teachings of Kabbalah. And each year, the numbers are growing!

• • • •

If you were inspired by this book in any way and would like to know how you can continue to enrich your life through the wisdom of Kabbalah, here is what you can do next:

Call 1-800-KABBALAH where trained instructors are available 18 hours a day. These dedicated people are willing to answer any and all questions about Kabbalah and help guide you along in your effort to learn more.

As Rav Yehuda Ashlag brought to the world
"the desire to influence," we have
so many opportunities in life to make choices every
day; to influence and transform ourselves,
our loved ones, the world.

This book is dedicated to the many Kabbalists throughout time, The Rav and Karen Berg, their family and
all the chevre, and teachers, who have deeply touched
my life and influenced the lives of so many people
around the world.

May the Light touch and influence the loves of my life:
my beloved children, Yitzchak Zev ben Avraham
and Necha Mariasha bat Avraham; my entire family
and all of my friends.